Machines That Build

by Whit Fisher
illustrated by John Rice

McGraw-Hill School Division
New York Farmington

Do you know what work is? The word *work* means different things to different people. For some, work might mean a job you go to every day. Other people say that thinking hard is work. An athlete might say that exercising is work. What do you think work is?

Scientists have their own definition of work. They say that work is done when a force changes the motion of an object. A scientist would say that pushing a box across the floor is work because a force is moving the box. What about pushing against a wall? If the wall does not move, then no work has been done. Any time you push or pull an object and change its motion, you are doing work.

Machines make it easier to do work. When you think of machines, you might think of the machines you see at a construction site. They do work because they lift, push, and pull other objects.

One kind of machine is a simple machine. Simple machines have very few moving parts.

One kind of simple machine is a lever. A lever is a bar that moves on a fixed point called a fulcrum. A seesaw is a kind of lever. On a seesaw, it is easy to move the other person up in the air. It would be very hard to lift that person yourself. The seesaw is a simple machine that makes lifting someone easier. A seesaw helps you to do work, even as you play!

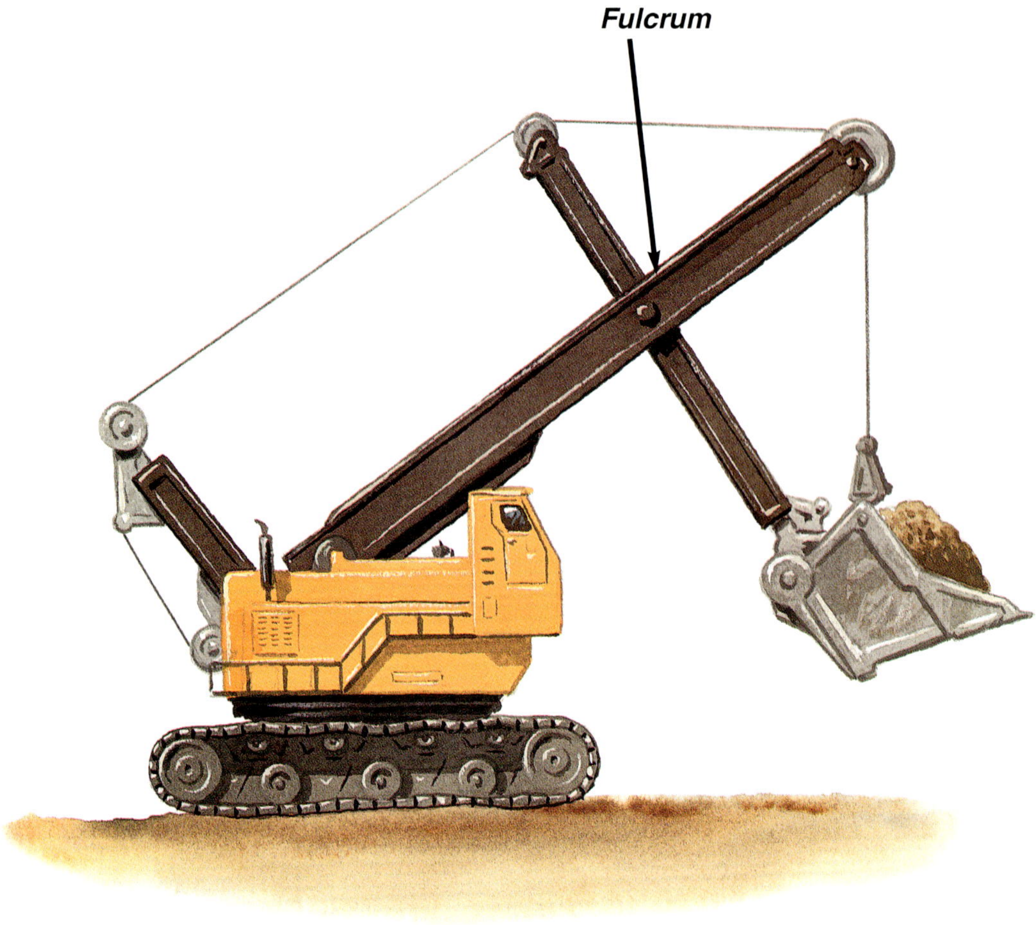

If you visit a construction site, you might see a power shovel. This big machine moves soil and rocks. It would take many people to do the work of one power shovel.

The power shovel uses a lever to help it lift heavy things. A big scoop is on the end of the lever. When the lever is lowered, the scoop fills with soil.

When the lever is raised, it moves up the way a seesaw does. The power shovel lifts soil instead of people, though. Then the power shovel can turn and drop the soil into a dump truck.

The dump truck works like a lever, too. The back of the truck moves on a fixed point, so it is easy to dump the soil. Can you see the lever? By using a lever, the truck can move the soil easily. Remember, work is using force to change the motion of an object.

Cranes are one of the oldest kinds of construction equipment. Some cranes use a lever to help lift heavy girders, or beams, high up in the air. These levers make it easier for the crane to lift and hold up a heavy weight. Here, a crane raises the girder to workers on a building. This way workers can get the heavy supplies they need to finish the building.

Another kind of simple machine is an inclined plane. An inclined plane is a flat surface that is raised on one end. A ramp is an inclined plane. This simple machine makes it easier to move things up and down. A ramp helps people in wheelchairs go to different floors of a building without using stairs.

At a construction site, you can see trucks driving up and down ramps. Many construction sites are on steep hills. Trucks would tip backward if they tried to drive straight up these hills. Inclined planes are cut into the hills. They let trucks go just as high, but over a longer distance. The ramps don't have to be steep. Trucks can climb them safely. These ramps are called switchbacks because they switch directions many times.

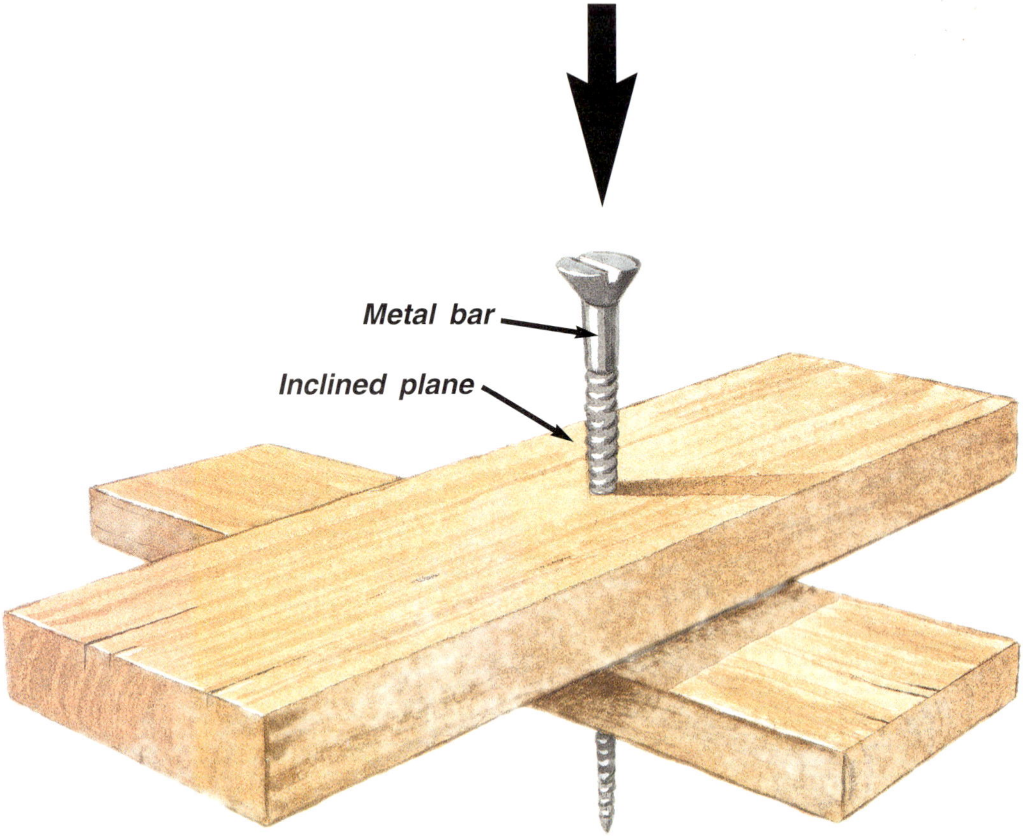

This screw has an inclined plane wrapped around a metal bar.

Construction workers use screws to hold boards together. Screws have lines, or threads, on them. The threads are an inclined plane that has been wrapped into a spiral. If you took the threads off of the screw, they would form a long, low inclined plane. The inclined plane makes it possible to twist the screw into wood. You apply force over a longer distance, just like any other inclined plane.

A pulley is another kind of simple machine. This machine can be used to do work by changing the direction of a force. Here we see a worker lifting a crate with a pulley. When the worker pulls on the rope, the rope turns on the pulley. The force now pulls up on the crate. This lets the worker pull up the crate and get it high above the ground.

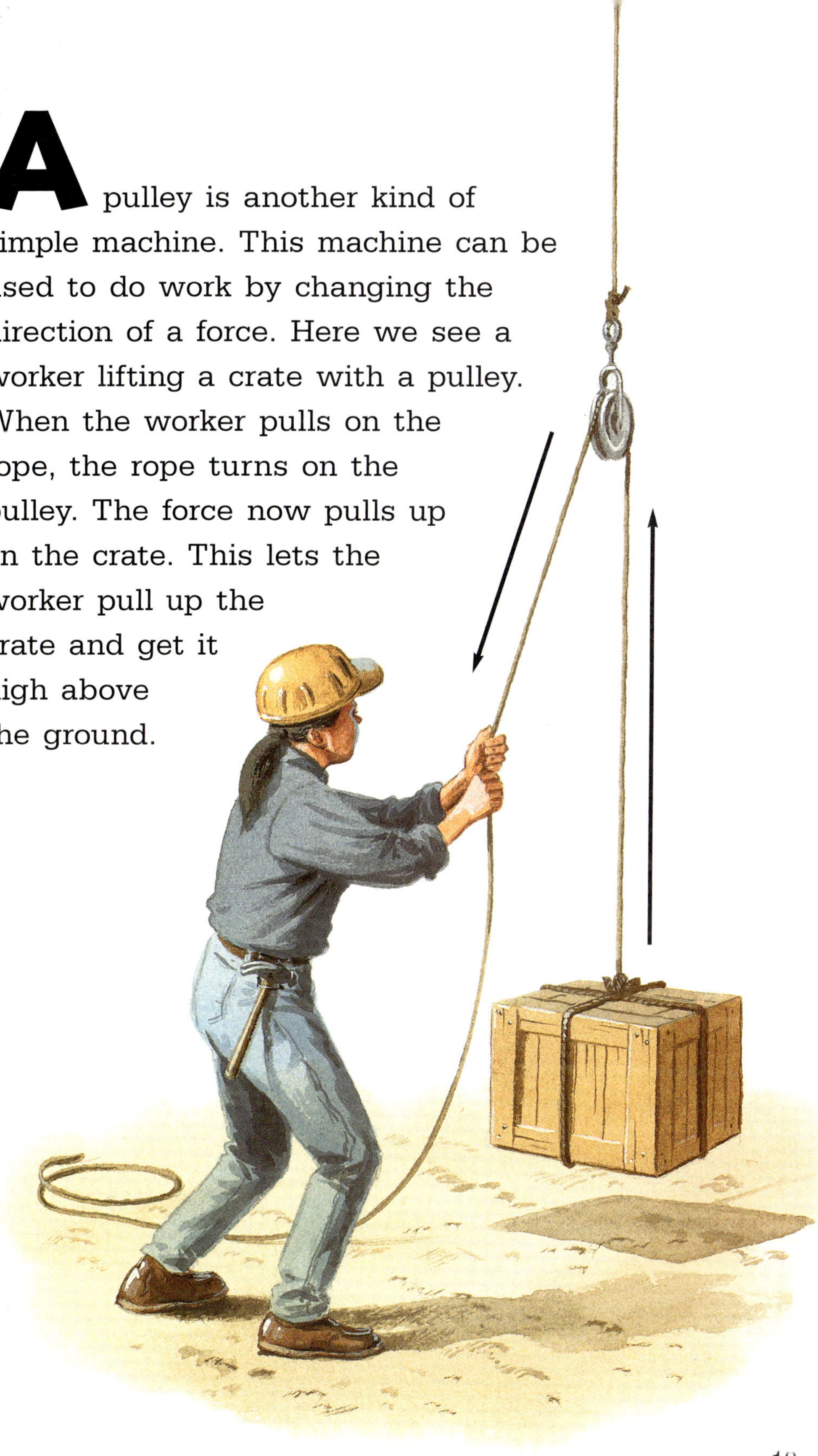

Power shovels also use pulleys. A cable pulls back toward the engine. This cable turns on a pulley to change the direction of the force. Now the force pulls upward, and can move the lever. This lets the power shovel lift up dirt.

A power shovel uses two simple machines: a lever and a pulley. This makes it a compound machine.

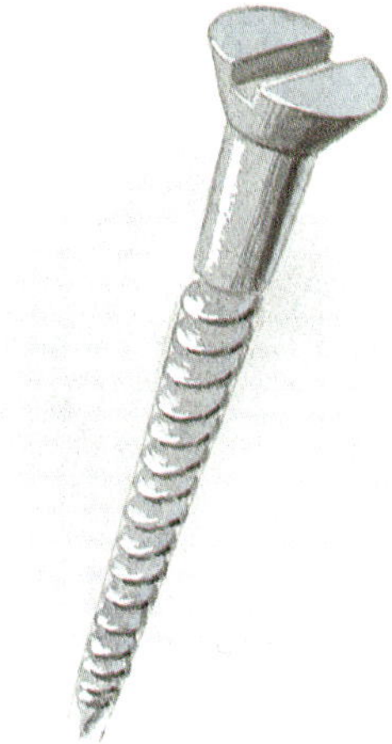

Everything you see here is a machine. Some, like the inclined plane, are simple. Some, like the power shovel, are compound. Some are powered by people. Others are powered by engines. You can probably find many machines in your house. They may look different, but they are all machines. Do you know why?

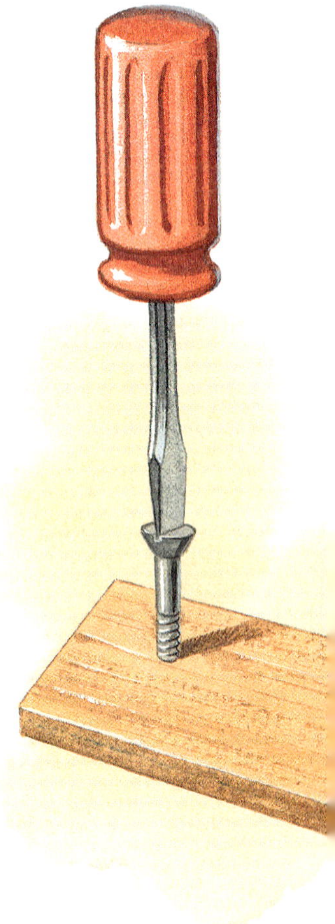

Machines help us to do work! They make it easier to lift, push, or pull things. They help us to build. They help us to travel. This book was made with machines. Your home was built with machines. Without machines, work would be much harder for everyone. By using machines, ordinary people can do extraordinary things.